W9-BXU-438

Dating and Sex

Defining and Setting Boundaries

By Judith Peacock

Consultant:
Jennifer A. Oliphant, MPH
Research Fellow and Community Outreach Coordinator
National Teen Pregnancy Prevention Research Center
Division of General Pediatrics and Adolescent Health
University of Minnesota

Perspectives on Healthy Sexuality

LifeMatters
an imprint of Capstone Press
Mankato, Minnesota

LifeMatters books are published by Capstone Press
PO Box 669 • 151 Good Counsel Drive • Mankato, Minnesota 56002
http://www.capstone-press.com

Printed in the United States of America

Library of Congress Cataloging-in-Publication Data
Peacock, Judith, 1942–
      Dating and sex: defining and setting boundaries / by Judith Peacock.
            p.   cm.—(Perspectives on healthy sexuality)
      Includes bibliographical references and index.
      ISBN 0-7368-0716-0 (hard cover) ISBN 0-7368-8845-4 (soft cover)
      1. Dating (Social customs)—Juvenile literature. 2. Sexual ethics for teenagers—Juvenile literature. 3. Interpersonal relations in adolescence—Juvenile literature. [1.Dating (Social customs). 2. Sexual ethics. 3. Interpersonal relations.] I. Title. II. Series.
      HQ801 .P348 2001
      306.73—dc21   00-009368
                                                               CIP

      Summary: Helps teens learn about dating relationships, includes discussion of healthy relationships, challenges couples face, making a decision about sex, and handling breakups.

Staff Credits
Rebecca Aldridge, editor; Adam Lazar, designer; Kim Danger, photo researcher
Production by Stacey Field

Photo Credits
Cover: ©Index Stock Photography/S W Production
©Artville, 15
©DigitalVision, 46
Index Stock Imagery/10, 23, 35, 40, 51, 55, 59
Photo Network/©Esbin-Anderson, 8, 31, 43; ©Tom McCarthy, 16
Unicorn Stock Photos/©Bill Bachmann, 6; ©Eric R. Berndt, 28
Uniphoto/©Bob Daemmrich, 18
Visuals Unlimited/©Jeff Greenberg, 32

A 0 9 8 7 6 5 4 3 2 1

Table of Contents

Chapter Overview

A dating relationship means that two people go out only with each other. They usually have strong feelings for each other.

Healthy dating relationships can offer several benefits, such as the opportunity to learn about sharing, commitment, and trust.

Dating relationships can bring risks as well. They can take a lot of your time and interfere with other activities.

Older teens with dating experience are more likely than younger teens without experience to benefit from dating relationships. Not every teen needs, or is ready for, a dating relationship.

A healthy dating relationship needs a solid base before it begins. A couple also needs to define and set boundaries before beginning a dating relationship.

Chapter 1

Deciding on a Dating Relationship

For most teens, dating, thinking about dating, or wanting to date is a big part of life. Dating occurs when two people go out together to have a good time. They may go out only once and never see each other again. If the people click, they may go out together many more times. They even may decide to commit themselves to a dating relationship.

What Is a Dating Relationship?

A dating relationship occurs when two people go out only with each other. They give serious attention to only each other instead of to several dating partners. People in a dating relationship usually have a strong attraction to each other.

Dating relationships are commitments. A commitment is a conscious decision that a relationship is important and valuable. It includes making an effort to keep the relationship. Teen dating relationships generally are short-term commitments that last a few months. However, some relationships last for a year or longer. Relationships even can lead to marriage. Although dating relationships among teens usually are fairly short, they tend to be intense and full of emotion. They also can be very meaningful.

A dating relationship is much the same whether the partners are straight, gay, or lesbian. A male attracted to other males is called gay. A female attracted to other females is called lesbian. A heterosexual relationship involves partners who are straight, or of the opposite sex. A homosexual relationship involves partners of the same sex.

Benefits of a Healthy Dating Relationship

Why be involved in a healthy dating relationship? It's fun to spend time with someone you really like and who makes you feel good. You have someone to do things with and someone to share your feelings and help you. A dating relationship can prepare you for a long-term commitment such as marriage. You learn about trust. You get to know what kind of person makes a good partner for you and what kind doesn't.

"Having a girlfriend sure took the hassle out of dating. I didn't have to spend time calling girls up and asking them out."—Paul, age 17

"The thing I didn't like about having a girlfriend was going to all her family's birthday parties and special dinners. I felt like I always had to play the part of the perfect boyfriend."—Alex, age 16

"It's great to have someone you can focus on completely. When you date one person for a long time, you can feel more comfortable sharing your feelings. You know you can trust him."

Katya, Age 16

Risks of a Dating Relationship

A dating relationship also has some risks. Having a serious boyfriend or girlfriend takes a lot of time and energy. The relationship may interfere with schoolwork, sports, or other activities. You may have difficulty meeting your goals. You may have less time to spend with family and friends. Focusing on one person may keep you from getting to know other people. There's a chance you could lose your own identity as you become a couple.

"I dated Lori for two years. It got to the point that everyone who saw me asked where she was. I finally realized that people thought of us as a couple and not as individuals. That bothered us, so we decided to make time to do more things apart."

Jeff, Age 17

Who Should Be in a Dating Relationship?

A dating relationship generally works best for older teens who have had dating experience. This experience helps teens decide the type of person with whom they want to have a committed relationship. Teens who are 13 and 14 years old usually have not had time to develop this experience. Group dating is a good way for younger teens to start learning about relationships.

Not every teen needs, or is ready for, a dating relationship. You may feel uncomfortable in a dating relationship. Many teens do not date at all during high school. Everyone has a different time schedule for forming relationships.

The Foundation of a Healthy Dating Relationship

A dating relationship should be a good experience for both partners. Before entering into such a relationship, ask yourself the following questions. Can you answer yes to all of them? If so, you will have a solid foundation on which to build a healthy relationship.

Do I know something about the person? Get to know the person before committing yourself to a relationship with him or her. Latching on to someone after only a few dates isn't a good idea.

Do both of us want the relationship? It takes two people to have a relationship. You can't have a relationship if only one person wants it.

Am I entering into the relationship for the right reasons? The right reasons would be because you like each other, want to be together, and enjoy each other's company. One wrong reason would be getting into a relationship just because everyone else is doing it. Other wrong reasons include starting a relationship because of pressure from friends or because you want to impress friends.

Do I have high self-esteem? You must feel good about yourself before you can care about another person. Teens with low self-esteem are more likely to be manipulated, or controlled, by their dating partner.

Am I being myself? Don't try to change yourself to get someone to accept you. Sooner or later your true personality and feelings will come out.

Defining and Setting Boundaries

Another important step before entering a dating relationship is to define and set boundaries. This includes answering questions such as:

How much time will I give to the relationship? Teens are busy with school, jobs, sports, and many other activities. You'll need to manage your time so that you can be with your partner and still meet other obligations.

How do I want to be treated? Partners in a healthy relationship treat each other with respect, care, and trust. Expect these things for yourself.

What do I want to gain from the relationship? You might want fun, friendship, or love. You might want to learn what it's like to be close to another person.

How far will I go sexually? Teens in a dating relationship often spend a great deal of time alone together, which eventually may lead to having sex. You need to plan ahead and decide how you will handle sexual situations. You need to talk about your decision with your partner.

Myth: Being in any relationship is better than being alone.

Fact: Thinking that any relationship is better than none can lead to getting stuck in an unhealthy relationship. It's important to be comfortable and happy alone.

Boundaries help guide a relationship. If you or your partner goes beyond the limits, you may need to reconsider your involvement with each other.

Points to Consider

What do you think are advantages and disadvantages of a dating relationship?

Is there pressure among your classmates to have a boyfriend or girlfriend? Explain.

Are you ready for a dating relationship? Why or why not?

Many people believe that young males are less willing than young females to commit themselves to a relationship. Do you think this is true? Why or why not?

Chapter Overview

A healthy dating relationship includes qualities such as caring, common interests, communication, equality, respect, and trust.

Partners in a dating relationship do not need to be in love. Over time, however, their relationship might grow into love.

The intense attraction at the beginning of a relationship is likely to be infatuation, or a crush.

Dating relationships that involve physical or emotional abuse are unhealthy. A partner who abuses alcohol or other drugs cannot contribute to a healthy relationship.

Chapter 2

What Is a Healthy Dating Relationship?

Dating relationships can be healthy or unhealthy. A healthy relationship makes you feel good and helps you grow as a person. An unhealthy relationship smothers and upsets you. It even may be unsafe.

Qualities of a Healthy Dating Relationship

A healthy dating relationship consists of many qualities. However, good looks, money, and the right clothes are not some of them. The important qualities include caring, common interests, communication, equality, respect, and trust. These qualities may be present at the beginning of a dating relationship, or they may develop later.

Caring

Partners in a healthy dating relationship care about each other's well-being. They try to help each other out. There is a mutual give-and-take. Partners show appreciation for each other.

Some couples are said to complement, or complete, each other. Where one partner may be talkative, the other partner may be quiet. Where one partner may like to do things on impulse, the other partner may like to plan activities. These couples often make a good match.

Common Interests

An old saying is that opposites attract. People who are the exact opposite sometimes do fall for each other. However, without common interests, two people usually won't stay together for long. Often, a relationship is fun if partners like doing some of the same things.

Communication

Partners in a healthy relationship communicate with each other. They feel comfortable and enjoy sharing the events of an ordinary day. They also can discuss difficult topics such as spirituality or politics. Partners are open with each other about their feelings and beliefs. They tell each other what they need. They also listen carefully to each other.

Equality

Equality is important in a dating relationship. This means neither partner monopolizes control. Neither partner acts like he or she owns the other. Each one values the other as an individual.

Respect

Partners in a healthy dating relationship respect each other. They don't put down each other's values, principles, goals, or opinions. They recognize their differences and don't try to change each other.

Trust

Trust develops over time in a dating relationship. Partners learn they can rely on each other's word. They can depend on each other to follow through on promises and commitments. They can tell each other anything and know that it won't be broadcast all over school.

"I dated Ellie for eight months last year. We were a great couple. In some ways we were alike. For example, we both thought school was important. In other ways we were different. Ellie helped me with my Spanish, and I helped her on the computer. We were there for each other but gave each other space. Fridays she went out with her girlfriends, and I hung out with the guys.

Dan, Age 18

"Ellie helped me face my emotions. I was angry with my mom for pressuring me about college. I never realized I was so mad at my mom for that until I talked with Ellie. When you spend a lot of time with one person, you really get to know her. And she helps you get to know yourself.

"Ellie and I still might be together, but she went away to college this fall. We both knew it would be too hard to keep up our relationship long distance. It even could have kept us from reaching our goals. But I know that Ellie and I will always be friends."

There are different kinds of love. In English, one word, *love*, is used to describe them all. There's:

Romantic love

Love between friends and family members

Love of country

Love for humankind

Love of ice cream, pizza, and other good things to eat

Love and a Dating Relationship

You may wonder: Do I have to be in love to be in a dating relationship? The answer is no. You should, however, like the person a great deal. Many dating relationships begin as friendships and grow into love.

Dating relationships may begin with infatuation, which people often mistake for love. Infatuation, or a crush, is a strong physical attraction to someone. Your heart might beat a little faster when you see the person. You may not be able to think of anyone or anything else.

Love is hard to define. It includes more than just the qualities for a healthy dating relationship. For example, love involves a person:

Who you know isn't perfect but care for anyway

Whose strengths and weaknesses you know and accept

Who could gain 30 pounds and you still would care for

Love takes time to develop. For right now, you don't need to decide if you are in love. Just enjoy your relationship. Your feelings will take care of themselves.

Unhealthy Dating Relationships

Some dating relationships are unhealthy. They even may be dangerous. Teens, and even some adults, often lack the experience and skills to deal with such relationships. Get out of an unhealthy relationship as fast as possible.

A relationship with a mean, possessive, or controlling person is unhealthy. These people often get angry when they don't get their way. They may put down their partner in front of other people or in private. They may want to know their partner's every move.

Extreme jealousy and possessiveness can lead to emotional and physical abuse. An abusive partner may yell at, slap, hit, kick, or even threaten to kill the other partner. This type of behavior should *never* be tolerated in a relationship. No one deserves to be treated this way.

A partner who abuses alcohol and other drugs cannot contribute to a healthy relationship. The person's relationship to the substance becomes more important than the relationship with his or her partner.

Dating and Sex

One in every three high school students is or has been in an abusive relationship. Extreme jealousy is the leading cause of dating violence.

Fast Fact

"I found out my boyfriend, Nate, was selling pot. I care about Nate a great deal, but I totally disagree with his actions. I tried to explain that what he was doing was dangerous and that he was risking messing up his future. Nate, though, cared more about selling drugs than about my opinion. I had to break up with him."

Kim, Age 17

Points to Consider

What would you add to the list of qualities needed for a healthy relationship?

Give an example of a couple showing care, equality, respect, and trust in their relationship.

Identify a couple who you think has a healthy relationship. What makes their relationship healthy?

What part should an attractive appearance have in a healthy dating relationship?

Chapter Overview

Developing a healthy dating relationship takes effort by both partners.

Partners need to spend time together to build a relationship. Too much togetherness, however, isn't healthy.

Each partner needs his or her own space. Having independent interests and keeping up friendships are ways to maintain separate identities.

Learning to communicate is essential for a healthy relationship. Couples also can learn techniques for solving problems.

Chapter 3

Developing a Healthy
Dating Relationship

A healthy dating relationship takes effort to develop and maintain. Both partners must contribute to the relationship. You and your partner can build your relationship in many ways. Spend time together, maintain independent interests, keep up friendships, learn to communicate, and learn to problem-solve. Keep in mind, however, that building a healthy dating relationship also requires time. You cannot push a relationship along. You need to be patient with yourself and your partner.

Spend Time Together

Spending time together allows you to learn more about each other. You should find out your partner's interests, likes, and dislikes. What are his or her goals and plans for the future? What is his or her family like? What experiences did he or she have early in life? How does your partner act around other people?

Balance and moderation are important in a relationship. This means not going overboard in one direction or another. For example, you don't want to help your partner so much that he or she becomes dependent on you. On the other hand, you don't want to ignore your partner's needs.

Time together doesn't always have to be a formal date. You don't always have to go somewhere such as a movie or restaurant and spend money. Instead, spend time together informally. Do your homework or eat a meal together at home. Help each other with household chores or do volunteer work in your community. Informal dates often let you see different sides of your partner's personality and character.

Have Independent Interests

While it's important to spend time together, too much togetherness is unhealthy. Having interests and hobbies outside your relationship is important. If you're always together doing the same thing, your relationship can become boring. You may find yourselves with nothing to talk about. Having independent interests helps to maintain your individual identity. It also allows you to learn new things from each other.

"When Kevin and I first met, we seemed **George, Age 17** to be real opposites. I was into theater, and he was all about sports, especially basketball. As our friendship grew, we began to learn from each other. Eventually, he taught me about the rules of basketball and gave me tips to improve my playing. I explained why being involved in theater meant so much to me. Now, he helps me read lines for auditions."

Keep Up Friendships

It's easy to neglect friends when you long to spend all your free time with your partner. However, try to find time to be with your other friends. Friendships usually last longer than teen romances. You may need your friends even more if you and your partner break up. Keeping up friendships also maintains your identity. Here are ideas for keeping in contact with friends:

Set up a special time to be with friends.

Return phone calls from friends.

Plan group dates with your friends.

Encourage your partner to keep up with his or her friends.

Tell your partner what you do with your friends and why they are important to you. This helps to prevent jealousy from creeping into your relationship.

Learn to Communicate

Communication is essential to a healthy relationship. You and your partner can learn techniques to help you share feelings and talk. Two good techniques are feedback and note writing.

Feedback

Breakdowns in communication often occur at the receiving end. One person says something, but the other person hears something different. Feedback can help prevent misunderstanding.

You may wonder what to do if your partner won't talk with you. Understanding the person's background may help prevent frustration. He or she may come from a family where talking about oneself is discouraged. Gender differences also may play a role. Many people believe that males are less talkative than females. You might get your partner to open up by asking him or her to choose a time to talk.

In feedback, the listener says what he or she thinks the speaker is saying. The speaker can agree or send the message again in a different way. Here's an example:

Ozzie: I thought I'd go to the game Friday night with the guys.

Alicia: What! Are you mad at me?

Ozzie: No. I just haven't seen my friends for a while. You could do something with your girlfriends while I'm at the game.

Note Writing

In note writing, partners write down their feelings and then exchange papers. The partners can react to and discuss what they read on each other's paper. This technique is useful when one partner has difficulty expressing feelings or when one partner tends to control conversation.

Learn to Problem-Solve

A dating relationship won't go smoothly all the time. Don't be afraid to risk speaking up if there's a problem. Speaking up is better than just hoping the problem will go away.

Arguments or disagreements will occur. Some arguing is healthy because it allows couples to get differences out in the open and work toward solutions. Being able to express differences openly and honestly shows equality in a relationship.

By following these rules, arguing can have positive results:

Attack the problem, not each other. Don't call each other names.

Stay in the present. Don't bring up past situations.

Avoid *you* statements, such as "You always . . ." or "You never . . ." Your partner may interpret these as put-downs.

Use *I* messages. For example, "I got upset when you didn't call. I thought you had decided to go without me." *I* messages can lead to problem-solving conversations.

Say what you want instead of what you don't want.

State the real issue and ask for feedback.

Negotiate, or discuss the problem to come to an agreement, and compromise.

Drop the discussion once a solution is found.

Points to Consider

How do you think a couple in a dating relationship should handle expenses such as the cost of a movie?

Give examples of inexpensive ways a couple could spend time together.

How much should you tell your friends about your dating relationship?

Chapter Overview

Common problems in dating relationships include jealousy, unreasonable expectations, feeling used, and cheating. Talking about these problems can help couples overcome them.

Problems also may develop when friends and family don't like a dating partner. Teens should listen to the opinions of other people and then decide for themselves what to do.

Teens who date people outside their race, cultural background, or religion may face special challenges. Gay and lesbian teens may need to overcome challenges as well.

Chapter 4

Challenges to a Dating Relationship

Developing a close relationship with another person is one of life's most satisfying experiences. It also is one of life's most challenging experiences. Sometimes problems occur that make building a relationship even more difficult.

Relationship Problems

People in a dating relationship may struggle with jealousy, unreasonable expectations, feeling used, and cheating. If you and your partner can recognize these problems, it's possible to overcome them.

Jealousy

Jealousy is a common problem in dating relationships. Jealousy is how you feel when you don't want to share a person. You may become upset if you see your partner looking at or talking with another boy or girl. You may feel jealous if your partner has a good time without you. Many arguments start with jealousy. Jealous feelings can cause a lot of misery.

Feelings of insecurity often lead to jealousy. An insecure person may doubt his or her ability to attract and keep a partner. Jealous feelings may lessen as the relationship grows and the person gains self-confidence.

There is no simple way to overcome jealousy, but you can lessen its hold on you. Making a list of your good qualities and talents may help you gain confidence in yourself. Talking with your partner about your feelings can help, too. Use *I* statements. For example, "I got upset when I saw you in the hall with . . ." Don't accuse your partner of anything. He or she may have done nothing wrong.

"My boyfriend, Rex, is captain of the hockey team. I got incredibly jealous of **Danika, Age 16** the attention other girls paid him. Sometimes after a game, Rex would ignore me and talk with other girls. I told Rex that I was feeling left out. He apologized and said he wasn't aware that he was ignoring me. He just felt he was being polite and friendly to the girls. After that, Rex made a special effort to include me. He introduced me to the girls, who usually just wanted to congratulate him after a good game."

"I've been going out with Wayne for a long time, and we're really close. The problem is he wants me to do things for him that I don't want to do—like his homework. I end up giving in because I'm afraid I'll lose him."—Annette, age 15

"My parents don't like my new girlfriend, Cindy, because she has purple hair and a nose ring. It doesn't matter that Cindy is an honors student. They still don't want me going out with her."
—Eddy, age 17

Unreasonable Expectations

People in a dating relationship often have unreasonable expectations. You should expect your partner to show you love, respect, attention, and courtesy. However, some expectations are not healthy or realistic. For example, you should not expect your partner to:

Be with you seven days a week. Both partners must have a life outside the relationship to make it work.

Promise to marry you. Even though you're serious, making a long-term commitment puts too much pressure on the relationship. Just let things develop at a normal pace.

Share every single detail of his or her life. There will be things you don't share with your partner and things your partner doesn't share with you. This is healthy and normal as long as the secrets aren't too deep and dark.

Feeling Used

In a caring relationship, couples help each other out. The helping should be mutual. Sometimes, however, you may find yourself doing more than your share. You may spend too much time on your partner's activities and neglect your own. As a result, you may begin to feel used and exhausted.

If you think your partner is cheating and you're in a sexual relationship together, use protection. This will help keep you from possibly getting a sexually transmitted disease (STD).

Think about why you give in to your partner's requests for help. Are you too eager to please? Do you fear rejection if you don't help your partner? You should want your partner to be with you because of who you are and not what you can do for him or her. You also should want a partner who is strong enough to take care of his or her own responsibilities.

Tell your partner in a kind, direct way that you need to spend more time on your own activities. Remind him or her that you sometimes need help and support, too. A caring partner will understand and apologize and accept the fact that you have your own life to live.

Cheating

Cheating can happen in different ways. It may include kissing another person or having sex with someone else. It even may include carrying on a romantic relationship with someone else via e-mail. If someone cheats on you, it's painful and you'll probably want to know why it happened.

The reasons people cheat vary. Some people may be bored with their current relationship. Others may be trying to make their partner jealous. Or, some may have found real interest in someone new. The only way you can be sure of a partner's reason is to ask. The answer, as well as his or her attitude, may help you decide if your relationship is worth working on. The decision is up to you because only you can decide what you are comfortable with.

Problems With Friends and Family

Friends and family may disapprove of a teen's dating partner. Their negative opinions can make dating partners feel uncomfortable or angry.

Friends

It's not realistic to expect all your friends to like your partner as much as you do. However, if many of them object to your relationship, take time to find out why. Listen carefully to what your friends say. Your friends care about you and don't want you to get hurt. They may see things about your partner that you don't see. Are you constantly making excuses for your partner or covering up for him or her? If so, something may be wrong with your relationship.

You may find that your partner treats you great but doesn't respect your friends. In that case, you will need to talk with your partner. Then you should be able to expect some changes in his or her behavior.

Family

Listen also to objections from your family. Before calling family members unfair, consider their side. Are they often right about things? Consider your reasons for dating your partner. Are you dating this person as a way of rebelling against your family? This isn't a good reason to be in a relationship.

Don't date someone behind your family's back. If you believe your partner is a special person, be persistent. Go over your partner's good points with your family members. Tell them the nice things he or she does for you. Ask your family to give your partner a chance. Invite your partner over more often so your family can get to know him or her. Ask your parents and other family members to do group activities with you and your partner. Your family probably will come to like your partner better.

Special Challenges

Teens in a dating relationship with someone of a different race, culture, or religion may face special challenges. They may have difficulty adjusting to their differences. People today are more accepting of mixed relationships than in the past. However, it's possible family and friends may not accept the relationship. People in the community may discriminate against the couple. That means people may be prejudiced against the couple and treat them unfairly.

If you're in a mixed relationship, you might do several things to meet these special challenges.

Talk with each other about problems you are likely to encounter. Decide ahead of time how you will deal with these problems. Try to think of positive ways to handle negative experiences.

Talk with family and friends about your feelings for your partner. The earlier you can involve them in your relationship, the more likely they will be to support you.

Learn about your differences. Try to find ways to share each other's culture. You might learn each other's language or participate in special celebrations together. Be aware, too, that you and your partner may come from backgrounds with different dating customs.

Homosexuality has existed in almost every culture and society, going back centuries. In some cultures, such as ancient Greece and certain Native American tribes, same-sex relationships were very acceptable.

Find friends who also are involved in mixed relationships. You share a special bond and can support each other.

Attend counseling sessions to learn how to deal with the challenges of a mixed relationship. These sessions may be available through a community center or a place of worship.

Gay and Lesbian Dating Relationships

Gay and lesbian couples may experience difficulty because of how others react to their relationship. Some people feel uncomfortable when they see same-sex couples in public. They may stare at gay and lesbian couples. Some may even make rude remarks. A few people with an extreme fear of gays and lesbians may try to hurt them physically. Such hostility can affect dating for gay and lesbian teens. It can make carrying on a dating relationship difficult and sometimes even dangerous. Gay and lesbian couples should still feel free to show their affection in public. It's important to be able to express yourself naturally. Just use good judgment.

Support groups and organizations provide a safe place for people in same-sex relationships. If you don't know where to find such places, you might want to ask a school counselor or supportive teacher. Gay and lesbian hot lines can help. Some communities have community centers, sports and social groups, and dances where teens can hang out.

"My girlfriend, Carly, and I go to a community center for gay and lesbian teens in our city. It's called District 107. It's a great place. Carly and I can be ourselves and be accepted. We can sit together, talk, hold hands, and hug if we want to, and no one harasses us. District 107 even had a gay and lesbian prom this spring."

Sharon, Age 17

Points to Consider

What would you do if you found out that your dating partner was cheating on you?

How could you help a friend who is having problems with a dating relationship?

What should you do if you don't like your partner's friends?

How are teens in mixed or same-sex relationships treated at your school?

Chapter Overview

Sexual intercourse within a healthy dating relationship can be very satisfying. However, sex does not have to be part of a dating relationship. Dating partners need to talk openly and honestly about the sexual part of their relationship.

Partners should consider several things when deciding whether to include sex in their relationship. They should think about the quality of the relationship, reasons for having sex, and possible risks.

Partners who are not ready for sex face the possibility of an unplanned pregnancy or a sexually transmitted disease. They also may face emotional stress, a changed relationship, and an uncomfortable situation.

Answering some questions honestly can help you and your partner decide if you're ready for a sexual dating relationship. Making a decision about sex isn't easy.

Chapter 5

Sex in a Dating Relationship

A healthy dating relationship may or may not include sexual intercourse. Sex is a possibility but not something couples have to do. Partners need to talk openly and honestly about the sexual part of their relationship. Each partner needs to consider the quality of the relationship and reasons for wanting or not wanting sex. They both need to think about the possible consequences of intercourse. Letting sex just happen is risky and can have unplanned consequences.

Reasons for Having Sex

Some reasons for having sexual intercourse are good. Some are bad. The good reasons occur within a mutually caring relationship. Sex in this setting can be a wonderful, pleasurable expression of love.

Good Reasons

Good reasons to have sex include wanting to experience pleasure, fun, and closeness. They also include wanting to express love and commitment and to relieve sexual tension and urges. Another good reason is to learn more about your body and what gives you pleasure.

"Beth and I have been going out for a while. **Chad, Age 18** I really care about her. We have fun together. We like the same things. And, we respect each other's opinions. We've started talking about having sex, and it feels all right to me. I think I'm ready. Even though we're not talking about getting married, the idea of us having sex feels good to me."

Bad Reasons

Bad reasons for having sex include wanting to repair a broken relationship or to hold on to your partner. Wanting to prove your love for your partner or wanting to please your partner aren't good reasons for sex, either. Another bad reason to have sex is to keep up with your friends.

"Things weren't going very well between **Jillian, Age 16** my boyfriend, Rob, and me. I thought that if we had sex, we'd grow closer. It didn't work out that way. All Rob wanted to do after that was have sex. He didn't want to talk or go out. We broke up a short time later."

Sexual intercourse poses risks for dating partners who aren't ready for it. These risks include unplanned pregnancy, sexually transmitted diseases, emotional stress, a changed relationship, and uncomfortable situations.

Unplanned Pregnancy

One risk of having sex is the possibility of pregnancy. This risk also exists if semen gets near the vagina, even without intercourse. Semen contains sperm, which are male sex cells. Dating partners may believe they would marry if the girl gets pregnant. In reality, 80 percent of teen fathers do not marry the mothers of their child. Even if the couple stays together and decides to raise the child, they can expect a difficult time. It takes energy, hard work, and money to raise a child. Teen parents may need to change their plans for the future.

Sexually Transmitted Diseases

Another serious risk of sexual intercourse is getting or spreading a sexually transmitted disease (STD). These diseases also are called sexually transmitted infections (STIs). Spreading an STD is a risk if one or both partners have had a previous relationship involving any sexual contact. An infected person can pass an STD during contact with the genitals, or sex organs. An STD also can be passed during vaginal, anal, or oral intercourse. Some STDs can damage a person's health permanently and even cause death. The symptoms of some STDs may not appear for several weeks, months, or years. A person may not be aware that he or she has or is passing on an STD.

Emotional Stress

Sexual intercourse involves the mind and emotions as well as the body. It can create intense feelings of joy and hurt, closeness and distance. These feelings can be overwhelming to a teen.

A Changed Relationship

Having sex can change a relationship. Sex often makes a relationship more intense. Couples may feel more tied to each other. They may find themselves headed for a long-term commitment they never intended. Sex may become the focus of their relationship.

Uncomfortable Situations

Dating partners need to consider how they'll feel if they have sex and then later break up. Will they be embarrassed if they run into each other again? Will they wonder what their ex-partner is saying to others?

Am I Ready for Sex?

The following questions can help you and your partner determine if you're ready to make sex a part of your relationship. The best way to take the test is for each of you to answer the questions separately. Then talk about the questions and your answers.

"Some kids jump too quickly into having sex. They figure if they can fall in love in a month, then they can have sex in a month, too."
—Twyla, age 16

1. Do my partner and I have a committed, mutually kind, and understanding relationship?... **Yes** **No**

2. Am I emotionally ready to handle a sexual relationship?.......................... **Yes** **No**

3. Do I have enough confidence in myself to share my body and my innermost thoughts and feelings with my partner?...................... **Yes** **No**

4. Do I want to have sex for pleasure, fun, and closeness and not because I feel pressured?...... **Yes** **No**

5. Do I know how pregnancy occurs?.............. **Yes** **No**

6. Do I know about STDs and how they're spread?.. **Yes** **No**

7. Do I know about reliable birth control and protection methods?.......................... **Yes** **No**

8. Am I going to use reliable birth control and protection every time I have sex?................ **Yes** **No**

9. Are my partner and I able to talk with each other about birth control and protection?........ **Yes** **No**

10. Does this decision fit with my values, morals, and goals?........................... **Yes** **No**

11. Is this something I really want to do?........... **Yes** **No**

Being intimate with another person can be wonderful. There are two kinds of intimacy, or closeness. Physical intimacy means having your body close to the body of your partner. Emotional intimacy means sharing your deepest thoughts and dreams and all your hurts. Emotional intimacy sometimes can be harder to achieve than physical intimacy.

Deciding About Sex

Deciding about sex isn't easy. You may feel pressure from peers and others to become sexually active. The media emphasizes sex, too. All the messages you get about sex can be confusing. Talk about sex with a parent or other trusted adult. Read books about relationships. Doing these things can help clear your thinking.

Talking With Your Partner About Sex

Talking with your partner about sex can be awkward and embarrassing. The closer your relationship, however, the easier it will be. One of you will need to get the conversation going. Here are a few tips:

Practice what you want to say.

Find a quiet place where you won't be interrupted.

Ask your partner for feedback.

When Partners Don't Agree

Both partners must want a sexual relationship. One partner may feel ready for sex while the other one doesn't. Partners in a healthy dating relationship respect each other's feelings. They don't pressure each other to do things they aren't ready for. Accepting differences is one of the things that makes a relationship healthy.

Points to Consider

Why is it important for dating partners to be honest with each other about their dating history?

Why do you think it's hard for many teens to talk about sex?

What is meant by the phrase "sex is not love"? What are ways couples can show love without having intercourse?

Chapter Overview

Partners in a dating relationship who decide to have sex must protect themselves from an unplanned pregnancy and STDs.

Two main groups of birth control are over-the-counter and prescription methods. Some over-the-counter birth control also may protect against STDs.

Partners in a dating relationship who decide to be abstinent must define the limits of their sexual activity.

Partners in a dating relationship can change their mind about sexual relations. They should let their partner know if something bothers them.

Chapter 6

Deciding About Sex

Teens who are dating may decide to include sexual intercourse in their relationship. Other dating partners may choose abstinence, or to avoid sexual intercourse. Whichever decision partners make, they must take responsibility for their choice. They must work to make their decision successful.

If You Decide to Have Sex

Couples who decide to have sexual intercourse must protect themselves against unplanned pregnancy and STDs. Both partners must take responsibility. If a couple can't talk about birth control and protection, they should think again about having sex.

Many methods of birth control are available. Two main groups are over-the-counter methods and prescription methods. A few over-the-counter methods also protect against STDs.

Over-the-Counter Birth Control and Protection

Over-the-counter birth control and protection can be purchased without a doctor's prescription. It's available in places such as drugstores and supermarkets. Over-the-counter birth control and protection methods are inexpensive and easy to use. They include male and female condoms, spermicides, and dental dams.

Male condom. This latex or soft plastic covering fits over the erect penis during vaginal, oral, and anal intercourse. Male condoms are 98 percent effective in preventing pregnancy when used correctly with every act of intercourse. Male latex condoms protect against certain STDs, including HIV. For this reason, they are strongly recommended for use with other birth control methods.

Female condom. This soft plastic pouch fits inside the vagina. The open end remains outside the vagina for the penis to enter. Female condoms are from 79 to 95 percent effective in preventing pregnancy. Their effectiveness in preventing STDs is not known. They may prove to be more effective than male condoms because they cover a wider area. The female condom also can be placed in the anus to provide protection from STDs during anal intercourse.

Spermicides. These include foam, creams or gels, suppositories, and contraceptive film. They are inserted into the vagina. Spermicides are not as effective as other birth control methods. They are best used as backup protection with male condoms, diaphragms, and cervical caps. Spermicides may provide some protection against certain STDs, but this needs more research.

Dental dam. This is a silky, thin latex material. Dental dams protect against STDs during oral-vaginal or oral-anal sex. A person can lick or kiss through the dam.

Prescription Birth Control

Prescription birth control must be obtained from a health care professional. Generally, a female first must have a pelvic exam. A pelvic exam is an examination of the reproductive organs. Prescription birth control includes birth control pills, Depo-Provera®, Norplant®, diaphragms, and cervical caps. None of these methods protects against STDs.

Birth control pills. When taken exactly as prescribed, birth control pills prevent pregnancy almost 99 percent of the time. They are convenient to use. Because they are drugs, birth control pills can cause side effects.

Depo-Provera. This is a birth control shot. Every 12 weeks, the female gets a shot in the arm or buttock, which is the fleshy part of the body where one sits. Depo-Provera is almost 100 percent effective in preventing pregnancy. Like birth control pills, it can cause side effects.

Norplant. This consists of six rubbery capsules. Each capsule is about 1 inch (2.5 centimeters) long. A doctor inserts the capsules on the underside of the female's upper arm. Norplant is nearly 100 percent effective in preventing pregnancy. Protection lasts for five years.

Diaphragm. This latex cup is worn inside the vagina during sex. A doctor or nurse fits a female with a diaphragm. It should be used with a spermicidal cream or gel to be most effective in preventing pregnancy. Without spermicide, a diaphragm is only 82 percent effective. With spermicide, this figure rises to 94 percent.

Cervical cap. A cervical cap is like a diaphragm, only smaller. It fits more tightly over the cervix than a diaphragm does. The cervix is the opening between the vagina and uterus. The uterus is the hollow organ where an unborn baby devlops. When used with spermicide, cervical caps are 91 percent effective in preventing pregnancy.

Getting Help With Birth Control and Protection

You can get help in deciding which method of birth control and protection is best for you. Talk with a parent or other trusted adult, a school nurse, or a family doctor. Your school might have a health center that can help. You also might visit a family-planning clinic. Look under *Clinics* or *Planned Parenthood* in the telephone book. The sections at the back of this book also contain helpful resources.

Your First Time

The first time you and your partner have sexual intercourse probably will be awkward and uncomfortable. For a girl who is a virgin, or who's never had intercourse, it may cause some pain. Developing a satisfying sexual relationship takes time. You and your partner must be patient and communicate with each other. You must tell each other what gives you pleasure.

"It took Jake and me a long time before we felt we were ready for sex. When we did decide, we wanted to do things right. A guy at a teen counseling center showed us how to use condoms, and we got some foam besides. My sister went away for the weekend, so she let us use her apartment. We didn't have to worry about being rushed or anyone walking in on us. Jake said we shouldn't worry about our performance but just relax. Afterward, we held each other close and talked and talked. It felt wonderful."

Michele, Age 18

If You Decide Not to Have Sex

Couples who choose not to have sexual intercourse must define what abstinence means to them. They must agree on boundaries, or limits, to their sexual activity.

Defining and Setting Boundaries

Sexual abstinence means no vaginal, oral, or anal intercourse. For some couples, it also may include avoiding any sexual activity that could lead to intercourse. Couples who are abstinent may choose not to do any of the following:

Hugging or kissing in a sexual way

Sexual touching above or below the waist

Mutual masturbation, or rubbing the genitals for pleasure

Body rubbing

Kissing the genitals

**"Here are just a few ways
I let my boyfriend know I love him:**

Make him a card for his birthday.

Give him a shoulder massage.

Put love notes in his locker.

Watch sports with him on TV.

Don't flirt with other guys.

Listen when he talks.

Don't be clingy or needy."

—Tonya, age 16

In deciding on boundaries, remember that two main reasons for choosing abstinence are to avoid unplanned pregnancy and STDs. If a male ejaculates near the outside of the vagina, sperm still could find their way into the female and cause pregnancy. Any exchange of body fluids such as semen, blood, or saliva could lead to spreading an STD.

"Tom is my first real boyfriend. We don't have sex because what we're looking for is **Roger, Age 16** a good relationship. Then we'll get into making love. That's the order we want it to go in."

How to Be Abstinent

Abstinence can be difficult when two people care about each other. You and your partner, however, can work together and support each other. You may find your relationship growing even stronger as you seek to remain abstinent. The following suggestions can help you stay abstinent. Join a support group and go on more group dates. Also, avoid situations that may lead to sex, such as being in dark, intimate places. Finally, set goals for your future.

A Special Relationship

Just because you and your partner have chosen abstinence doesn't mean that you can't show love for each other. There are many ways to express love other than intercourse. Give each other smiles, kisses, hugs, and back rubs. Go for long walks, share a romantic dinner, or talk for hours on the phone. There are a thousand ways to be emotionally and physically close to each other!

Changing Your Mind

Couples who have had sexual intercourse can change their mind. Abstinence always is a choice. Couples who are abstinent may change their decision, too. If they decide to have sex, they should be ready with birth control and protection.

Points to Consider

Whom would you go to for advice on dating and sex? Why would you choose that person?

What are other ways besides sexual intercourse that couples can show they care for each other?

What advice would you give a friend who is thinking about having sex for the first time?

Chapter Overview

Dating relationships end for many reasons. Teen relationships often break up because dating partners grow and change in different directions.

Some people stay in unhappy relationships because they are afraid of breaking up. Staying in a relationship that is not working is a mistake.

It's important to get out of an abusive relationship.

Honesty and sensitivity can make a breakup less painful. However, feeling sad and lonely after a breakup is natural. You can learn to let go and move on.

Chapter 7

Handling a Breakup

Many teen romances last only a short time. Teens who begin a dating relationship shouldn't expect a lifetime commitment. However, breaking up with someone can be very painful. It's possible, however, to learn to let go and move on.

Reasons for Breaking Up

Couples break up for many different reasons. The romance may have gone out of the relationship. Partners may be unable to overcome differences in values or lifestyles. One partner may feel used or abused by the other partner. People change and grow in different directions. This is a major reason for the breakup of teen relationships.

"I wanted to break up with Ashley, but I didn't have the guts to do it. I started acting like a jerk so she'd break up with me. It worked, but now I wish I'd done things different. Ashley deserved better treatment than that."
—Lloyd, age 15

Fears About Breaking Up

Some people fear breaking up with a dating partner. They may fear being alone or being rejected. They may not want to hurt their partner's feelings. In some cases, the person may be afraid of getting hurt physically. People sometimes get stuck in a relationship because they're afraid of breaking up.

It is a mistake to stay in a relationship that's not working. It's not fair to you or to your partner. Neither of you will be happy. Remember that it takes two people to have a relationship. If one of you doesn't want to be in the relationship, the relationship won't work.

If You Are the One Who Wants to Break Up

You may be the one who wants to break up. You can handle the breakup in a way that will be sensitive to your partner's feelings.

Tell your partner face to face. Don't write a letter or send a friend to tell your partner. Don't just stop answering your partner's phone calls. An exception to a face-to-face meeting might be if you are in danger of being hurt physically.

Find a quiet time and place to talk. Don't break up in front of friends.

Plan what you will say. Don't list the person's bad points or try to make yourself look like the good person.

Make a clean break. Don't give false hope of getting back together.

Be kind and respectful. If you're interested in someone else, don't brag about your new relationship.

Try not to feel guilty about breaking up. Your "ex" may be hurt now but later on may realize that you did the right thing.

If Your Partner Wants to Break Up

Your partner may be the one who wants to break up. If you do not want to end the relationship, you may feel rejected and depressed. Being "dumped" doesn't mean you are any less special. It just means the relationship wasn't working. Think of all the good things you gained from being together. You can take what you learned into your next relationship and grow from the experience.

If the Breakup Is Mutual

Both you and your partner may want to call it quits. Agree to meet and tell each other why you think you should break up. That way you each will have a clear understanding of what happened. If you decide to remain friends, be sure to define what you mean by the word *friends.*

How to handle bumping into your ex:

If you're with a group of friends, walk up and say hello. Try to have fun, but don't seem like you're trying too hard.

If you're with a new dating partner, introduce your date to your ex. Don't start talking about old times, or your date may think you want your ex back.

If you see your ex with a new dating partner, give them both a friendly hello. Avoid acting mad or upset. Otherwise, your ex may think you're jealous.

"Jenny was my girlfriend for three years. When we split, we wanted to stay friends. We knew this could be tricky, so we made some rules.

Nick, Age 18

"Rule 1. No contact—not even a phone call—for 30 days. This gave us a chance to get used to not being a couple anymore.

"Rule 2. No talking about new boyfriends or girlfriends. It's still easy to get jealous, even if the relationship is over.

"Rule 3. No telling our friends the details of our breakup. This helped prevent gossip.

"Rule 4. No dating each other's best friends. We agreed this would feel strange, like being betrayed.

"These rules helped Jenny and me go from romance to friendship. I'm glad, because I trust and respect Jenny and want her in my life."

The Question of Getting Back Together

Many times either one partner or both partners find it hard to let go. You might talk about getting back together. Ask yourself some questions. Are you meeting each other's needs? If not, are you both capable of meeting those needs? What areas of your relationship need compromise? Are you both willing to make those compromises? The relationship didn't work as it was—that's why you broke up. You need to talk about how you both can work together to make changes for the better.

Breaking Free From an Abusive Relationship

You may need to break up with an abusive partner. You may or may not want to try talking face to face with the person. Keep your safety in mind. Don't begin a conversation about breaking up when you're being attacked. Wait until the person is calm and go to a place with other people around. Explain what your partner has done to push you away. State the facts coolly and clearly.

The person may refuse to accept your decision or threaten to hurt you. Tell your parents or another trusted adult. These people can help you take action to protect yourself.

After a Breakup

After a breakup, you may feel sad and lonely. This is natural. You have experienced the loss of someone close to you. You need time to grieve your loss and heal. However, when a relationship breaks up, some teens go through deep depression. They feel hopeless—as if nothing matters anymore. For these teens, a broken romance even may trigger thoughts of suicide, or killing themselves. Teens who feel this way need to talk about their feelings and get help.

Letting Go and Moving On

You can do several things to help yourself get over a broken relationship.

Talk about your grief with someone close to you. If your sadness doesn't begin to lift after a few weeks, you may need to talk with a counselor.

Spend time with friends. Your friends can help cheer you up and make you feel good about yourself.

Keep busy. Go back to old hobbies or start new ones. Get involved in a sport. Look for volunteer opportunities in your community.

"After I broke up with Warren, I spent 10 minutes each day writing in my journal. I jotted down all my feelings about our relationship. My journal writing helped me understand why things fell apart. It made the past easier to leave behind and the future simpler to plan. I saw things I didn't want to repeat in a future relationship."

Kathlyn, Age 17

Being Alone

You can use the time following a breakup to get to know yourself better. Many people find that they enjoy their own company. Everyone needs time alone to think and relax.

Starting to Date Again

When you're ready to start dating again, let people know. Not everyone may realize you're available. People may be used to seeing you with your ex-partner. Go with one or two friends to parties, basketball games, or the mall. People soon will learn that you and your partner are no longer together.

Be open to new relationships and experiences. Don't try to find someone who is exactly like your ex-partner. Don't try to find someone who is the total opposite, either. It's good to look for certain qualities in a dating partner. However, you might cheat yourself by passing up someone who doesn't fit your concept of the perfect partner.

Beware of rebound relationships. This means don't jump into another serious relationship with the first person you start dating again. Create some space between your last relationship and your next. This way you're likely to choose someone using both your heart and your brain.

Points to Consider

Your friend feels blue following the breakup of a six-month dating relationship. How could you help your friend?

What tips do you have for handling the breakup of a dating relationship?

How would you tell a dating partner that you wanted to break up?

Glossary

abstinence (AB-stuh-nuhnss)—choosing not to have sexual relations

abuse (uh-BYOOSS)—physical or emotional mistreatment

boundary (BOUN-duh-ree)—limit placed on something

commitment (kuh-MIT-muhnt)—a conscious decision that a relationship is important and valuable

communication (kuh-myoo-nuh-KAY-shuhn)—the act of sharing information, ideas, or feelings with another person

feedback (FEED-bak)—comments and reactions to something

genitals (JEN-uh-tuhlz)—the sex organs

infatuation (in-fach-yoo-AY-shuhn)—a feeling of being wildly attracted to or in love with someone; having a crush on someone.

intimacy (IN-tuh-muh-see)—closeness

mutual (MYOO-choo-uhl)—shared

relationship (ri-LAY-shuhn-ship)—the way in which people get along together

self-esteem (self-ess-TEEM)—a feeling of personal pride and respect for yourself

sexual intercourse (SEK-shoo-wuhl IN-tur-korss)—penetration of the penis into the vagina, anus, or mouth

sexually transmitted disease (STD) (SEK-shoo-wuhl-lee transs-MIT-tuhd duh-ZEEZ)—a disease that is spread through sexual contact between people

For More Information

Endersbe, Julie K. *Teen Sex: Risks and Consequences.* Mankato, MN: Capstone, 2000.

Kirberger, Kimberly. *On Relationships: A Book for Teenagers.* Deerfield Beach, FL: Health Communications, 1999.

Peacock, Judith. *Abstinence: Postponing Sexual Involvement.* Mankato, MN: Capstone, 2001.

Peacock, Judith. *Birth Control and Protection: Options for Teens.* Mankato, MN: Capstone, 2001.

Stewart, Gail B. *Gay and Lesbian Youth.* San Diego: Lucent Books, 1997.

Useful Addresses and Internet Sites

Planned Parenthood Federation of America
810 Seventh Avenue
New York, NY 10019
1-800-669-0156
www.plannedparenthood.org

Planned Parenthood Federation of Canada
1 Nicholas Street, Suite 430
Ottawa, ON K1N 7B7
CANADA
www.ppfc.ca

Sexuality Information and Education Council
of the United States (SIECUS)
130 West 42nd Street, Suite 350
New York, NY 10036-7802
www.siecus.org

drDrew.com
www.drdrew.com
Provides advice and articles on relationships
and sexual issues that affect teens and young
adults

Sex, Etc.
www.sxetc.org
Contains articles on sexuality written by teens
for teens

Teen Advice Online
www.teenadviceonline.org/dating
Provides a variety of articles about dating for
both guys and girls

teenwire
www.teenwire.com
Gives teens information on sexuality and
relationships

Domestic Violence Hot Line
1-800-799-SAFE (800-799-7233)

IYG (Peer support for gay, lesbian, and
bisexual youth)
1-800-347-TEEN (800-347-8336)

Kids Help Phone in Canada
1-800-668-6868 (Canada only)
http://kidshelp.sympatico.ca

Index

Index continued

DATE

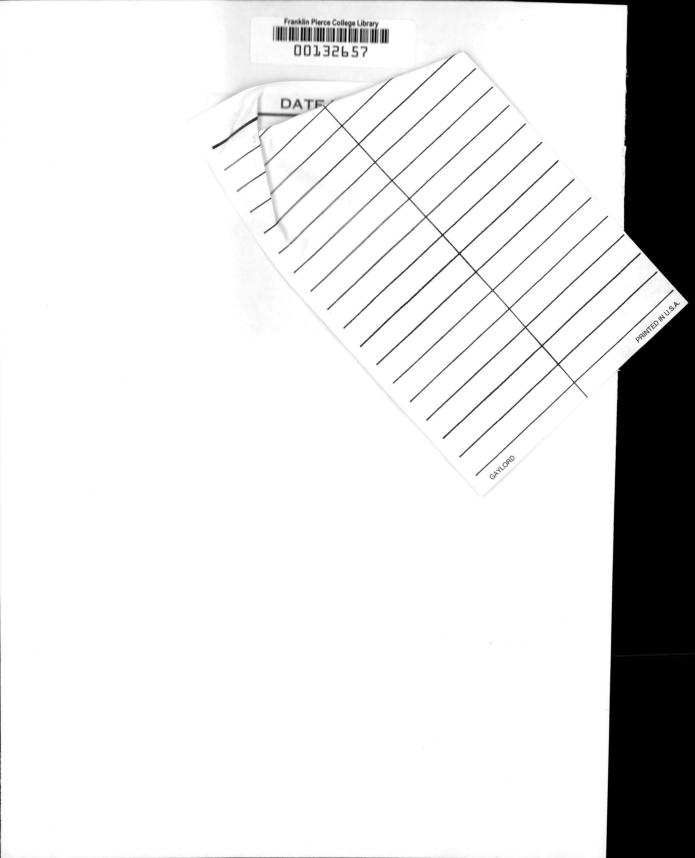

GAYLORD

PRINTED IN U.S.A.